Mother Goose

TELLS
THE TRUTH

ABOUT

MIDDLE
AGE AND BEYOND

A Collection of Wise and Witty Poems for Adults

By Sydney Altman   Illustrated by Marty Riskin

Published by
BaBoom Press, Inc.
79 Woodchester Drive
Newton, MA 02467
Tel: 617-332-9254

Illustrations by Marty Riskin   www.martyriskin.com

Graphic design by Creative Solutions, Inc.   www.allcreativesolutions.com

ISBN: 978-0-9707275-3-4

Printed in Hong Kong by Kwong Fat Printing
Fourth printing, revised edition 2008

Let's face it, while getting older is no joke, laughing about it certainly makes it easier.

To order books and funny products, see our new comic inventions, and even contribute some of your own aging humor,

... visit us at
www.SecondHalfLaughs.com

For my parents, Harry and Shavee Altman,

And to Baby Boomers everywhere.

This book belongs to:

_____

CONTENTS

CONTENTS

The Original Inspirations ... page 66

Said Baby Boom Babies
It's time to take stock,

We're too young to get old
We're still rock 'n' roll jocks.

This is all a mistake,
Misconceptions must fall.

The truth is over fifty,
Is the best age of all.

1

Have you seen
the Lipo man,
the suction man,
the surgeon man?

Have you seen
the Lipo man
who works on
Sunset Lane?

Yes I've seen
the Lipo man,
he suctioned my can,
It's now flat as a pan.

I can highly recommend
the Lipo man
who works on
Sunset Lane.

This baby boomer plays the market,

This baby boomer sells by phone,

This baby boomer drills and fills teeth

… and this baby boomer works at home.

But this baby boomer,
    Still a child of the Sixties,
Grows weed in his geodesic dome.

Jack tried to be nimble.
He tried to be quick.

He shot hoops with young guys
And ruptured a disc.

Oh where, Oh where
has my estrogen gone?
Oh where, oh where
can it be?

I was once young and fair
Now I sprout facial hair
Oh hormones please
come back to me.

5

Botox, Botox, has FDA approval,
To instantly perform the job
of wrinkling removal.

Who'd have thought a poison
When diluted to the max,
Could teach my facial muscles
The right way to relax.

And I'll stick with my treatments
They make my skin so yummy,
Plus if I ever stop them
I'll look like a museum mummy.

He got a divorce.
He showed no remorse
He married his young thing
As a matter of course.

He put rings on her fingers.
She painted her toes.
His ex has the kids,
You know how that goes.

Ms. Peep spent a heap
Her beauty to keep
Her skin she did tuck and hem.

Leave your money alone
So you'll look like a crone:
Rich old women attract younger men.

Hippity, Dippity, Rock,
 I camped out at Woodstock.
But the songs now in style
 Are exceedingly vile,
I am in a complete state of shock.

9

Tinkle, tinkle in a jar
Yearly check-up here you are.

My LDL is much too high
I'm sure my pressure's reached the sky.

Why's his finger up so far?
I wish I'd never left my car.

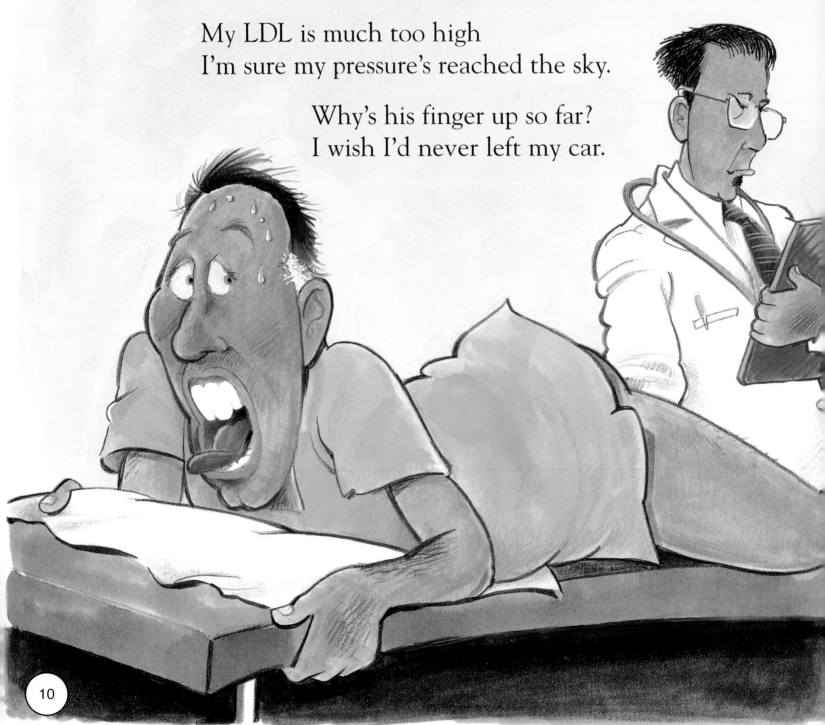

Jack and Jill
   Jogged up the hill,
      Their breath came
         faster and faster.
Before the top
   They made a stop,
      Narrowly averting
         a myocardial disaster.

Mr. Simon was a thigh man
Now he's in despair.
No more pats and winks at work,
Harassment's in the air.

Said in-house counsel to Mr. Simon,
"Lawsuits we can't have any."
Said Mr. Simon to the lawyer,
"I was only being friendly."

Low-fat cake, no-cal shake
    South Beach man,
        I've tried every diet
    From here to Japan.

I've poached it, I've steamed it,
    I've drunk herbal tea.
        I think from now on
    I'll just let myself be.

Middle-aged Molly
   on the rock climbing wall,
Prayed to herself that she
   wouldn't just fall.

"I took up this sport to be
   supple and fit,
But frankly, at my age,
   I'd just as soon sit."

Mr. Jack Horner
    Stood on the corner,
Watching the young girls go by.

When he was younger
    He had sexual hunger,
Now he just feasts with his eyes.

We're the post-war generation,
A bulge within our nation.

So do as you're told,
Don't tell us we're old.

I tried to log on,
My mouse I did click,
But using computers
Is making me sick.

Men these days lead such merry lives For they can have so many wives.

First wife gets them through their school,

Next wife has children as a rule,

Third wife makes them feel so young,

Fourth wife gives them an old-age son,

Fifth wife sees them to their grave, And then runs off with the money they saved.

Ding Dong Bell,
My hearing's shot to hell.
I'm no longer thin,
Don't know what's out or in.

I now hold books far out
To read what they're about.
I bulge in places I was flat
What am I to make of that?

That age has done my body harm,
But hasn't stolen all my charm.

I do not like thee managed care,
For now I know I've not a prayer
Of getting the treatment that I need
No matter how I beg or plead.

By phone, I'm told by this stupid man,
"That isn't covered by your plan."
He suggests that I pay out-of-pocket.
Does he want me to take my house and hock it?

HMOs it's you I loathe.
Have you ever heard of the Hippocratic Oath?
Don't you know that providers are supposed to care?
Whatever happened to Dr. Kildare?

Rita, Rita, Prozac Eater,
had a friend
and couldn't keep her.

My friend, she said,
detests all pills,
while I know they're
the cure
for society's ills.

22

Our heads are in a whirl,
Cause our teen-aged boy and girl,
Have homework we must finish in their stead.

They've explained that if they could,
They'd complete it, yes they would,
But if they do, they might as well be dead.

Do we want them to have no friends?
Well, between Facebook and IMs,
It takes hours to maintain the social quo.

Don't we know that those who don't blend
Often come to bad ends,
At least they do get up for school and go.

If wishes were horses I'd take a long ride,
Away from demands that tug at my side.
I'd ride long and hard
And I would ride steady,
And wouldn't come home
Until good and ready.

I once was such a leftist guy,
There was no cause I didn't try.
Joined SDS, burned my draft card,
Tried to blow up Harvard Yard.

Maturity has cleared my sight,
I now see things in a different light.
I understand that laws are good,
They protect my funds and my neighborhood.

I vote for conservative candidates
And refuse to engage in political debates.

A middle age riddle:
I now often piddle
And my figure resembles a spoon

Yet I still have a yen
For sex now and then,
But it's young girls who make
    the men swoon.

I'll tell you another:
　　I've turned into my mother,
　　　　Something I swore not to do.

It's very unnerving
　　To get dressed in the morning
　　　　And see your mom staring right back at you.

An
aged primipara
On a reproductive spree:
Three kids under six
At age forty three.

She fed them
and changed them
And kept them well read,
And by seven at night
They put her to bed.

O h damn it, Oh blast it!
I've lost my reading glasses.
   I left them here a minute ago,
   So how come I can't find them?

            Can't find them, can't find them,
            Can't read a thing without them.
               It's bad enough I'm going blind,
               Do I also have to lose my mind?

A buyer, a shopper,
A label name-dropper,
What makes you feel like heaven?

Dot-com, dot-com,
It's changed my life
I now shop 24/7.

Mary had a lot of lamb
A lot of spam, a little ham,
Mary had two pints of jam
Her spirits were so low,
And every time she felt depressed
To the fridge she'd go.

She's joined Weight Snatchers,
And she knows
She's breaking every rule.
She dreads next weigh-in
With her gain
She'll feel like such a fool.

32

A man name of Morty
A few years past forty
Questioned the meaning of life.

Clad just in pajamas
Went to the Bahamas,
Leaving his children and wife.

33

Websites, Blogs and E-mail
through the Internet I sail.
Communication's now a wonder
though it's torn my world asunder.

I still remember when I'd go
to the mailbox … it was slow.
But I'd whistle while I ambled,
and my brain, it felt less scrambled.

34

Pussy cat, pussy cat
How I would preen,
    When I was young
    The catcalls were obscene.

Now that I'm older
No one is there,
    Wherever I go
    I get nary a stare.

I wrinkle, I crinkle
　　I no longer twinkle,
　　　　How did this come so soon?

Just yesterday I was thirty-one
　　I'm sixty-three next June.

Stock market, stock market
   I'm down on my knees,
You've got to recover
   I'm begging you, please.

I'd gotten used to easy cash
My wife and I had quite a stash.

Stock market, stock market
   please go higher
If you crash we can never retire.

My bladder's gone crazy, dear Doc,
I'm up around the clock.
Every time I fall asleep
I have to take a leak.
Do you think it's my prostate, oh Doc?

A.A.R.P.
Do you take me
for a fool?

People, when
they're fifty
Don't retire
as a rule.

For male menopause
Let's hear some applause,
It's about time that men
    paid the cost.

They were feeling so smug
Now let them take some drug
To restore those hormones
    they've lost.

Our SUV must sell it quick,
  Because it is making our planet sick.

We must get a hybrid, efficient and small,
  To reduce our dependence on foreign oil.

But we were so happy sitting so tall,
  We had room for four kids, a large dog and beach ball.

When we trade in our car we will have to downsize
  Should the dog or a kid go, please kindly advise.

MEADOW Muffin
Mall

41

Gen-Mart, Gen-Mart, can I buy a clone?
One of me or maybe one of someone better known.

Or maybe I should simply clone my aging dog named Firth,
I truly love him dearly and he's not long for this earth.

It's such a tough decision; which clone should I choose?
I haven't had such problems, since the last time I bought shoes.

Your breasts and butt
    are falling down
Falling down, falling down.
Your breasts and butt
    are falling down,
My poor Sadie.

Exercise will lift them up,
    lift them up, lift them up.
If you believe that bunk
    you're out of luck,
My poor Sadie.

43

"My wife and I share equally,"
Said this guy named Cort.
"She does the house, her job, the kid
And I give her my full support."

44

A mild-mannered man, name of Clyde,
Went in search of his male sense of pride.

He read Robert Bly
And beat drums with some guy,

And felt he'd been took for a ride.

Osteoporosis
Please leave me alone
For I've grown attached
To my every bone.

"I took her to bed"
    Crowed thirtyish Ned,
        "I love the chase you know."

"Enjoy while you can"
    Said sixtyish Dan,
        "You'll soon be running slow."

My college reunion's coming.
I can't imagine that
It's been so long since I left school.
I can't go looking fat.

I wonder who has made it big?
And who became a mother?
I've changed my mind
Won't go at all,
I hated school,
Why bother?

I once had a tushie
So high and so round

Now that I'm older
It falls towards the ground.

I've been making no sense
My memory's gone bye.
I pause for words
It's so absurd
And here's the reason why.
Since I've started aging
My brain has lost its zing,
At the rate my cells are dying
I soon won't know a thing.

I have these conversations with my spouse,
His name is Sonny
We can't remember what we've said,
I'm glad you think it's funny.
Just because you're younger
And can still quote some good prose
Time will catch your neurons too,
By fifty they'll have froze.

Our children, our children have all left our home,
Through their empty rooms we gleefully roam.

But we fear that they'll tire of independence
And return home to us,
They hate paying those rents.

Middle-aged Stu
 Go watch some porn
   Your libido is shorn
     Your wife is forlorn.

And where is our Stu
   Who could make young girls weep?
     He's under the covers,
       Fast asleep.

53

A tosser, a shaker
A 4 A.M. waker,
What keeps you up at night?

It's getting used to getting old,
An all too common plight.

I once was so hip,
Even dropped LSD.
So how come my kids
Are much cooler
than me?

I'm an aging woman
Rather short and stout,

I get told I'm acting crazy
When I sing and dance about.

But now that I am older,
And quite over my self-doubt,

I do anything I feel like,
I just let it all hang out.

The pill worked, my wife sleeps, she's satisfied,
While I'm wide awake and just terrified.

Because my erection stands tall as a crown,
It's over four hours and it will not go down,

I need some help fast but I wish that I knew
When I get to my doctor, what he plans to do.

What are aging boys
   made of?
What are aging boys
   made of?
Love handles galore
And a proneness
   to snore
That's what aging boys
   are made of.

What are aging girls
   made of?
What are aging girls
   made of?
Impaired memories
And dread thigh-
   spread disease
That's what aging girls
   are made of.

I'm having a mid-life crisis,
It makes me scream
and shout.

If and when
I'm young again
You'll never see me pout.

59

When I was young I thought that I'd
See the world before I died,
I wouldn't care which way I went
I'd live on scraps, sleep in a tent.
Now I'm older and while I'd still like to roam,
If I can't afford a good hotel I'll just stay home.

Sane Jane
let her hair go gray.

If folks don't like it
they can stay away.

61

Poor Mrs. Fifty
Was not feeling nifty,
Eating her low-fat Swiss cheese.

When she was twenty
She used to eat plenty
And never gained weight
round her knees.

There once was a woman
Who lived in a burb:
Full-time job, Full-time kids
And a hubby named Herb.

She tried very hard
To do everything right
And frequently thought about
Hopping a flight.

63

Monday's child is full of face,

Tuesday's child has lost some grace,
Wednesday's child now takes things slow,
Thursday's child sometimes feels low.
Friday's child is tired of giving,
Saturday's child is re-thinking her living.

But each has decided
Through a middle-aged haze
That, given the choice,
They'd like many more days.

In Case You Were Wondering ...
The Original Inspirations

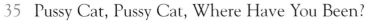